YOUR KNOWLEDGE HAS VALUE

- We will publish your bachelor's and master's thesis, essays and papers

- Your own eBook and book - sold worldwide in all relevant shops

- Earn money with each sale

Upload your text at www.GRIN.com and publish for free

Natalie Cohen

Positive psychology and psychotherapy: How do they influence the treatment of cancer?

GRIN Verlag

Bibliografische Information der Deutschen Nationalbibliothek:

Die Deutsche Bibliothek verzeichnet diese Publikation in der Deutschen National-
bibliografie; detaillierte bibliografische Daten sind im Internet über http://dnb.d-
nb.de/ abrufbar.

Imprint:

Copyright © 2013 GRIN Verlag GmbH
Druck und Bindung: Books on Demand GmbH, Norderstedt Germany
ISBN: 978-3-656-49243-6

This book at GRIN:

http://www.grin.com/en/e-book/232001/positive-psychology-and-psychotherapy-
how-do-they-influence-the-treatment

GRIN - Your knowledge has value

Der GRIN Verlag publiziert seit 1998 wissenschaftliche Arbeiten von Studenten, Hochschullehrern und anderen Akademikern als eBook und gedrucktes Buch. Die Verlagswebsite www.grin.com ist die ideale Plattform zur Veröffentlichung von Hausarbeiten, Abschlussarbeiten, wissenschaftlichen Aufsätzen, Dissertationen und Fachbüchern.

Visit us on the internet:

http://www.grin.com/

http://www.facebook.com/grincom

http://www.twitter.com/grin_com

Positive Psychology And Psychotherapy:

How Do They Influence The Treatment Of Cancer?

University of Groningen
Date: 09.05.2013

Natalie Cohen

Abstract

That a positive attitude and psychological support can promote the therapy of cancer and even encourage the cure is a widely held view. In this paper the capabilities and limitations of positive psychology and psychotherapy will be discussed with the aid of two studies. The first one has laid the foundation for this research area and the second study replicated the latter using a more appropriate methodology. It will be shown that some assumptions made in recent decades are not more than parts of a myth, which is progressively dissolved by high quality studies.

Positive Psychology And Psychotherapy: How Do They Influence The Treatment Of Cancer?

In 1989 Spiegel and colleagues, have published one of the first and still frequently cited studies that reports a relationship between the attendance of breast cancer patients in in-group psychotherapy and their survival time (Spiegel, Bloom, Kraemer & Gottheil, 1989). Since then, many studies with similar results (e.g. Fawzy et al., as described in Coyne, Stefanek & Palmer, 2007) were released. Other researchers and even an entire area in psychology, namely positive psychology, believe apart from this life-prolonging effect in positive outcomes like a better quality of life (Colby & Shifren, 2013) or an improved adjustment to cancer (Mark & Meyer, as described in Helgeson, Cohen, Schulz & Yasko, 2001), which can allegedly be achieved through a positive attitude or psychological intervention. Those assumptions became popular among the general population in the last decades and influence therefore not only the attitude of cancer patients toward their disease, but also the expectation of other people towards the patients.

Since there is not only support for the impact of positive psychology and psychotherapy on the cure and therapy of cancer, but also more and more critical studies and meta-analyses of previous studies, the question of the effectiveness and importance of intervention for the patients will be discussed in this paper. To begin with, the advantages of a positive attitude and psychotherapy for cancer patients are discussed, followed by a description of Spiegel and colleagues' popular study. The points of criticism will be presented and a comparison will be provided by a study, which does not support the above-described point of view. This discussion should provide a basis to show that the assertions of positive psychologists and supporter of psychotherapy's positive affect on cancer cure are a myth without sufficient evidence and information, cancer patients and their families can not rely on.

Advantages of psychological intervention and a positive attitude

In the literature about a positive attitude and psychological support for cancer patients several advantages are repeatedly mentioned. Like already described above, cancer patients who report optimism also tend to have a better quality of life (Colby & Shifren, 2013). In addition they are likely to cope better with their disease. The optimism and a positive attitude enables cancer patients to give their otherwise frightening and daunting disease a meaning, which in turn strengthens their fighting spirit and intrinsic goal to overcome the disease (Aspinwall & Tedeschi, 2010). Other effects of a positive attitude are "positive health behaviours, better recovery from certain medical procedures, positive changes in immune system functioning, and improved survival rates" (Aspinwall & Tedeschi, 2010).

The psychological support through group therapy should have similar advantages. Especially stressed patients can learn how to cope properly with their disease (Goodwin et al., 2001). By providing more information about the disease, the issue becomes normal for the patients and therefore increases the self-esteem and the ability to deal with it (Helgeson et al., 2001). Through the exchange of experiences and provided support by the other group members, cancer patients do not become socially isolated and feel that they are not left alone (Spiegel, Bloom, Kraemer & Gottheil, 1989). Some patients learn to ask for more analgesics, thus pain control is improved (Goodwin et al.). Since the treatment of cancer has a great impact on the self-esteem of the patients as the result of visible side effects of the chemotherapy or surgeries, group intervention could help the patients in form of downward comparison (Helgeson, Cohen, Schulz & Yasko, 2001). On the one hand the patients see that they are not the only ones suffering and on the other hand that there are other patients who are more effected. Moreover the educational part of group intervention is important.

Spiegel and colleagues' study about psychological treatment of cancer patients

As noted above, Spiegel and colleagues' study, which was published 1989, is one of the most popular studies in this area. The researchers were one of the first who believed to show that psychological treatment of cancer patients has a prolonging effect on their survival. To prove this, they created an intervention and a control group. The participating women had all metastatic breast cancer and were referred to the study by their oncologists (Spiegel et al., 1989). Overall 30 out of 50 women survived long enough and consented to participate in the study for one year. In the control group 24 women took part (Spiegel et al.).

The therapy consisted of group meetings, where the patients talked about how to cope with cancer, about their feelings and physical problem and about pain control (Spiegel et al.). The patients in the control group received the regular oncological care, but did not take part in a group therapy. Spiegel and colleagues found out that the patients who received psychological treatment survived twice as long as the patients in the control group. Interestingly, immediately after the year of treatment, the survival rates in the intervention group were lower. The researchers explain that the significant differences have shown up eight month after the year of psychological treatment, because the effects are mild and have to cumulate. As an explanation for the longer survival, the social support through the group was emphasized, especially because more unmarried patients attended in the intervention group and, according to Spiegel and colleagues, those usually do not survive a long as married patients. Further explanation was provided through the mobilization of the patients' resource (Spiegel et al.), for example by improving the diet or pain control. Some researchers also see a link between the immune system and the emotional state (Kennedy et al., as described in Spiegel et al.), but there is not sufficient evidence for this.

The points of criticism regarding Spiegel and colleagues' study

A lot of studies, which investigated the relationship between positive psychology or psychological therapy and the progression of cancer, are of low methodological quality (Petticrew, Fraser & Regan, 1999). Spiegel and colleagues' study is one of them. To begin with, survival is not a primary end point of the study (Coyne, Stefanek & Palmer, 2007), which is usually requested in a clinical trial. The reason for this is that the survival-prolonging effect was unexpected and has been noticed after the conduct of the study, which actually only should have examined the effect on psychological outcomes. Another issue concerns the measurement of the survival time. Because of the existing or possible variance in samples like theses, the usage of the median instead of the mean is more common. Indeed, when the median survival time for Spiegel and colleagues' samples was calculated, there was a difference of only two months instead of the stated 18 months (Sampson, as described in Coyne et al.). This means that after using another, more appropriate measurement, the outcomes were not statistically significant anymore. The significance is in addition questionable because of the small sample sizes, which provide a low power and contribute to the risk of a type one error (Pressman & Cohen, 2005).

Beside the statistical deficiencies of the presented study, there are also possible biases that could have distorted the results. Firstly, the non-psychological treatment of the patients was not controlled. The treatment patients could have been encouraged through the group to seek other or more medical treatment. Thus, there might be a co-intervention confound, which makes a proper comparison with the control group impossible (D.J. Cook et al., as described in Coyne et al., 2007). The randomization of the patients into the control and intervention group might be biased, too (Coyne et al.). More patients were assigned to the treatment group and their staging at initial diagnosis favoured them (Spiegel et al.). Finally, it is important to describe and adjust baseline characteristics of the treatment and control group in order to judge about the effect that should be measured. Otherwise it is impossible to exclude possible confounding variables (Petticrew, Fraser & Regan, 1999). This was not provided in the presented study. In conclusion, although the study of Spiegel et al. is popular and often cited, there are biases and statistical mistakes, which call the reliability of the study into question.

Common biases in this research area

Besides co-intervention bias, too small sample sizes, a low methodological quality and insufficient randomization that were described in relation to Spiegel and colleagues' study, there are other biases that do not only concern the studies, but also the quality of meta-analyses and the general knowledge of this topic (Petticrew, Fraser & Regan, 1999). Case control studies, which often support the described myth, are affected by recall bias. As Petticrew and colleagues stated in their meta-analysis about the relationship between adverse life-events and risks of breast cancer, reports that negative life events contributed to the outbreak of the disease may "simply be a result of the illness". That is, cancer patients might look for a cause for their disease and relate therefore to negative life events. This is supported by the fact that registry studies, which are not dependent on subjective reports, do not report such a relationship as case control studies (Petticrew et al.). Other possible biases in subjective reports are reporting bias and perceptional distortion (Rasmussen, Scheier & Greenhouse, 2009).

Another bias, which also had an impact on the popularity of the myth that psychotherapy and a positive attitude can stave off cancer, is file drawer bias (also: publication bias). Studies that represent a statistical significance in their result and that correspond with the common belief in our culture are more likely to be published (Pressman & Cohen, 2005). This bias is retrieved in the media's role as distributer of the myth among the general population.

The media's influence on the knowledge of the general population regarding positive psychology and psychological intervention in cancer patients

Since the media is the main source of knowledge regarding health and new medical findings, it has a great impact on the general population. Headlines like "Stress and cancer link confirmed by scientists: A direct link between stress and cancer has been confirmed by scientists for the first time." ("Stress and cancer link confirmed by scientists", 2010) or public statements of celebrities support the misbeliefs that are diffused by the media. An example is the professional cyclist Lance Armstrong, who made his battle against cancer public. He described "how he felt that he expelled the cancer cells from his body" (Coyne, Tennen & Ranchor, 2012), giving other cancer patients the feeling that they are not fighting enough if they remain ill. Such stories also raise the expectations hold by the relatives and friends of the patients regarding their attitude. Despite the lack of evidence that a positive attitude will help to survive, cancer patients are supposed to be optimistic and show fighting spirit. Another problem, which was already mentioned above, is the publication bias. The journalists' knowledge is limited and might not tell the whole truth (Entwistle, 1995).

Goodwin and colleagues study as a comparison to the study of Spiegel et al.

To provide a positive example of a study that examines the effect of psychosocial support on survival, Goodwin and colleagues (2001) study will be discussed now. The study was conducted with the attempt to replicate Spiegel and colleagues' study with the exception of a better methodology. The goal was to proof whether psychological support by groups will affect the survival time. To start with, larger sample sizes were used. Spiegel et al. started with 86 patients, while Goodwin et al. sampled 235 cancer patients. There were strict criteria the patients had to meet, e.g. life expectancy of more than three month and the ability to speak and read English.

Before the intervention started, the baseline characteristics of the patients were described to make a proper comparison between the control and experimental group possible. Moreover the end points of the study, namely survival and psychosocial functioning, were determined. This was one of the missing features in Spiegel and colleagues' study, although it is common in clinical studies. The patients in the intervention group took part in group meetings of the same length and regularity as in the study described previously. The control group did not receive any psychological support of this kind. Overall the methodological quality of this study is higher than of Spiegel et al.'s study since the deficiencies were eliminated. Goodwin and colleagues report a power of 99 per cent to find an improvement in survival of the same extent as the comparison study. Nevertheless, no significant difference in survival time was identified between the experimental and control group. Psychological benefits were only statable for women who were particularly distressed. In conclusion, one can say that after improving the quality of Spiegel et al. study from 1989, which reported significant effects of psychological interventions for cancer patients, none of those could be proven.

Arguments against positive psychology and psychotherapy regarding cancer patients

So far the advantages of a positive attitude and psychotherapy were described thoroughly. Since it was stated at the beginning of this paper that it is a myth that they have an influence on the cure or therapy of cancer, the disadvantages and concerns will be now clarified. The misbelief that a negative attitude and adverse life events cause or exacerbates cancer influences many patients. Wang and colleagues observed that about 30 per cent of female cancer patients believe that stress and worry are the cause of their disease (Wang, Miller, Egleston, Hay & Weinberg, 2010). This may give the patients the illusion that they have control over the cancer with the consequences of despair and depression when they realize that they cannot influence it, e.g. by changing their life style. Cancer patients have to cope with a lot of things and the assertion that their disease is self-inflicted burdens them even more.

Cancer patients who attribute cancer to stress are more likely to practice yoga and meditation after the diagnose (Panjari, Davis, Fradkin & Bell, 2012). Besides the illusion that they can influence the progress of the disease on this way, the patients are also willing to pay and invest time in order to alter their life style. As Stefanek et al. stated, this is "disrespectful of patient time, resources" (Stefanek, Palmer, Thombs & Coyne, 2009). Moreover, one should consider that the demands to attend at weekly group meetings, yoga lessons and the like are too high for an ill person. Studies like Goodwin and colleagues' observed that those efforts might not have benefits for everyone, e.g. patients who are not overly distressed or that have a decreased self-esteem after participating in a group therapy. Despite the allegation that the self-esteem could be improved through downward comparison, the contrary had occurred in studies (Coyne, Stefanek & Palmer, 2007).

Another aspect in this discussion is that the absence of pessimism has more effects on mental health than the presence of optimism (Colby & Shifren, 2013). Furthermore, the trait of positive affect is considered to be a stable one and thus is not easily manipulated (Pressman & Cohen, 2005). Ultimately, the golden mean between exaggerated optimism and pessimism, namely realism, might be the best way to cope with cancer. On this way, the patient can have the fighting spirit, group support and mobilization of resources that are described in connection to a positive attitude and psychotherapy, but they still do not underestimate the potential threats and seriousness of cancer nor do they have the illusion that they could control their cure.

An overall conclusion and suggestions for future research

Positive psychology and psychotherapy might have a positive affect on cancer patients, but most studies that try to prove it are methodologically questionable and should not be taken into account as evidence. In addition, there are more and more researchers, who held an opposite opinion that is established on high-quality studies. This paper shows that, despite a few advantages, the myth that has been created by the media and by the insufficient application of critical thinking by researchers, who citied and distributed false assumptions, can be harmful for their patients and their environments.

Since many studies that have been conducted in the recent years show which benefits psychotherapy can have, one should dedicate future research to the actual cause. Recent studies state that it is more the lack of pessimism than the optimism that influences the mental health of patients. This path should be further pursued.

References

Aspinwall, L. G., & Tedeschi, R. G. (2010). The value of positive psychology for health psychology: progress and pitfalls in examining the relation of positive phenomena to health. . *Annals of Behavioral Medicine, 39*(1), 4-15.

Colby, D. A., & Shifren, K. (2013). Optimism, mental health, and quality of life: A study among breast cancer patients. *Psychology, Health & Medicine, 18*(1), 10-20.

Coyne, J. C., Stefanek, M., & Palmer, S. C. (2007). Psychotherapy and Survival in Cancer: The Conflict Between Hope and Evidence. *Psychological Bulletin, 133*(3), 367-394.

Coyne, J. C., & Tennen, H. (2010). Positive psychology in cancer care: Bad science, exaggerated claims, and unproven medicine. *Annals of Behavioral Medicine, 39,* 16-26.

Coyne, J. C., Tennen, H., & Ranchor, A. V. (2012). Positive psychology in cancer care: a story line resistant to evidence. *Annals of Behavioral Medicine, 39,* 35-42.

Entwistle, V. (1995). Reporting research in medical journals and newspapers. *British Medical Journal, 310,* 920-923.

Helgeson, V. S., Cohen, S., Schulz, R., & Yasko, J. (2001). Group support interventions for people with cancer: Benefits and hazards. In A. Baum & B. L. Andersen (Eds.), *Psychosocial interventions for cancer* (pp. 269–286). Washington, DC: American Psychological Association.

Goodwin, P. J., Leszcz, M., Speca, M., Hunter, J., Ennis, M., Koopmans, J., et al. (2001). The effect of group psychosocial support on survival in metastatic breast cancer. *The New England Journal of Medicine, 345*(24), 1719-26.

Panjari, M., Davis, S. R., Fradkin, P., & Bell, R. J. (2012). Breast cancer survivors' beliefs about the causes of breast cancer. *Psycho-Oncolgy, 21,* 724-729.

Petticrew, M., Fraser, J. M., & Regan, M. F. (1999). Adverse life-events and risk of breast cancer: A meta-analysis. *British Journal of Health Psychology, 4*(1), 1-17.

Pressman, S. D., & Cohen, S. (2005). Does positive affect influence health?. *Psychological Bulletin, 131*(6), 925-971.

Rasmussen, H. N., Scheier, M. F., & Greenhouse, J. B. (2009). Optimism and physical health: a meta-analytic review. *Annals of Behavioral Medicine, 37,* 239-256.

Spiegel, D., Bloom, J. R., Kraemer, H. C., & Gottheil, E. (1989). Effect of psychosocial treatment on survival of patients with metastatic breast cancer. *The Lancet, 2,* 888-91.

Stefanek, M. E., Palmer, S. C., Thombs, B. D., & Coyne, J. C. (2009). Finding what is not there: Unwarranted claims of an effect of psychosocial intervention on recurrence and survival. *Cancer, 115*(24), 5612-16.

Stress and cancer link confirmed by scientists. (n.d). In Mirror News. Retrieved January 14, 2010, from http://www.mirror.co.uk/news/uk-news/stress-and-cancer-link-confirmed-by-scientists-194755

Wang, C., Miller, S. M., Egleston, B. L., Hay, J. L., & Weinberg, D. S. (2010). Beliefs about the causes of breast and colorectal cancer among women in the general population. *Cancer Causes & Control, 21*, 99-107.